ENDANGERED CHIMPANZEES

Bobbie Kalman & Hadley Dyer

🌳 Crabtree Publishing Company

www.crabtreebooks.com

Earth's Endangered Animals Series
A Bobbie Kalman Book

Dedicated by Hadley Dyer
For Fred and Eileen Dyer, with love.

Editor-in-Chief
Bobbie Kalman

Writing team
Bobbie Kalman
Hadley Dyer

Substantive editor
Kelley MacAulay

Project editor
Kristina Lundblad

Editors
Molly Aloian
Reagan Miller
Kathryn Smithyman
Niki Walker

Design
Margaret Amy Reiach

Cover design and series logo
Samantha Crabtree

Production coordinator
Katherine Kantor

Photo research
Crystal Foxton

Consultant
Patricia Loesche, Ph.D., Animal Behavior Program,
Department of Psychology, University of Washington

Illustrations
Katherine Kantor: back cover, pages 5, 14
Bonna Rouse: page 19

Photographs
Minden Pictures: Gerry Ellis: page 13 (bottom);
   Frans Lanting: page 7
Naturepl.com: Karl Ammann: page 29;
   Anup Shah: page 18 (bottom)
Steve Robinson/NHPA: page 26
Visuals Unlimited: Fritz Polking: page 28
Other images by Corel, Creatas, and Digital Vision

Crabtree Publishing Company

www.crabtreebooks.com   1-800-387-7650

Copyright © **2005 CRABTREE PUBLISHING COMPANY**.
All rights reserved. No part of this publication may be
reproduced, stored in a retrieval system or be transmitted in
any form or by any means, electronic, mechanical, photocopying,
recording, or otherwise, without the prior written permission
of Crabtree Publishing Company. In Canada: We acknowledge the
financial support of the Government of Canada through the Book
Publishing Industry Development Program (BPIDP) for our
publishing activities.

Cataloging-in-Publication Data
Kalman, Bobbie.
  Endangered chimpanzees / Bobbie Kalman & Hadley Dyer.
    p. cm. -- (Earth's endangered animals series)
  Includes index.
  ISBN-13: 978-0-7787-1859-8 (RLB)
  ISBN-10: 0-7787-1859-X (RLB)
  ISBN-13: 978-0-7787-1905-2 (pbk.)
  ISBN-10: 0-7787-1905-7 (pbk.)
  1. Chimpanzees--Juvenile literature. 2. Endangered species--
Juvenile literature. I. Dyer, Hadley. II. Title.
  QL737.P96K2539 2005
  599.885'168--dc22   2005000348
                                                      LC

**Published in
the United States**
PMB16A
350 Fifth Ave.
Suite 3308
New York, NY
10118

**Published
in Canada**
616 Welland Ave.,
St. Catharines, Ontario
Canada
L2M 5V6

**Published in the
United Kingdom**
73 Lime Walk
Headington
Oxford
OX3 7AD
United Kingdom

**Published
in Australia**
386 Mt. Alexander Rd.,
Ascot Vale (Melbourne)
VIC 3032

Contents

Endangered chimpanzees

Chimpanzees or "chimps" are **endangered** animals. In the past, chimps were found in 25 African countries. Today, chimpanzees can be found only in about 21 African countries. Sadly, the chimps in half of these countries may soon become **extinct**. They face many threats in the **wild**, or the natural places where they live.

Words to know

Scientists use certain words to describe animals that are in danger. Some of these words are listed below.

vulnerable Describes animals that may soon become endangered

endangered Describes animals that are in danger of dying out in the wild

critically endangered Describes animals that are at high risk of dying out in the wild

extinct Describes animals that have died out or that have not been seen in the wild for at least 50 years

What are chimpanzees?

chimpanzee

gorilla

orangutan

Chimpanzees are **mammals**. Mammals are animals that have backbones. They are **warm-blooded** animals. The body temperatures of warm-blooded animals stay about the same, no matter how hot or cold their surroundings are. Baby mammals **nurse**, or drink milk from the bodies of their mothers. Most mammals have fur or hair on their bodies.

Great apes

Chimpanzees belong to a group of animals called **primates**. The largest primates are **great apes**. Chimpanzees, gorillas, bonobos, and orangutans are great apes. All great apes are endangered.

Two types of chimps

There are two main **species**, or types, of chimpanzees: common chimpanzees and bonobos. This book is about common chimpanzees.

Four groups

Today, scientists believe that there are about four groups of common chimpanzees— Western chimpanzees, Central chimpanzees, Eastern chimpanzees, and Nigerian chimpanzees. Each group of chimps lives in a different part of Africa.

Bonobos are sometimes called pygmy chimpanzees. They are also endangered.

Chimpanzees in danger

Western chimpanzees and Nigerian chimpanzees are the most endangered common chimpanzees. All four groups of chimps may be extinct within 50 years, however.

Scientists **estimate** that there are fewer than 100,000 chimps in the wild, but it is hard for scientists to know the exact number. Animals in the wild are often difficult to find, so it is hard for scientists to count them.

Chimpanzee communities

Chimpanzees live in communities that include dozens of chimps. Each community is made up of smaller groups of chimps. The smaller groups change often because chimps from different groups spend time together.

Young female chimps that are ready to **mate** and have babies often leave their communities to join other communities. After having babies, some females return with their babies to live with the communities into which they were born.

Top chimp

Each community is led by the most powerful male chimp. He is called the **dominant** male. To keep his position as the leader, the dominant male must show that he is the strongest chimp in the community. He shows his strength by putting on **displays**, such as running around and making noise.

A new leader

Younger male chimps may try to become the dominant male in a community. The young chimps challenge the dominant male. They put on displays to show that they are stronger than he is. If one of the young chimps shows that he is the most powerful, he becomes the new leader.

When a male chimpanzee puts on a display, he is noisy and very active. His fur stands up to make his body look as large and as strong as possible.

9

Chimpanzee homes

Most chimpanzees live in African **rain forests**. These hot, rainy forests are the **habitats**, or natural homes, of chimps. The thick forests are filled with large trees and many kinds of plants and animals.

Swing time

Chimpanzees spend some of their time on the ground, but they often climb up tall trees. They move around in the trees by **brachiating**. Brachiating is swinging from branch to branch using the arms.

Home sweet home!

Each chimpanzee community has its own **home range**. A home range is the area of land in which a community lives and finds food. The male chimps in a community spend much of their time guarding the borders of their home range against males from other communities.

A place to sleep

At night, chimps build nests for sleeping. They choose safe spots in trees and make their nests by weaving together parts of plants such as leaves, twigs, and branches. The nests are shaped like bowls. This shape makes the nests perfect for curling up and sleeping!

The only chimps that share nests are mothers and their babies.

A chimpanzee's body

Chimpanzees have black hair all over their bodies, except on their faces, ears, the palms of their hands, and the soles of their feet. Baby chimps have pink skin, but it becomes darker as the chimps grow older.

Males are bigger

Male chimps are slightly larger and heavier than are female chimpanzees. The average male chimpanzee is about four feet (1.2 m) tall and weighs over 100 pounds (45 kg). The average female is less than three-and-a-half feet (1 m) tall and weighs less than 100 pounds (45 kg).

Knuckle-walking

Chimpanzees use their hands and feet for walking. They walk on the soles of their feet and the knuckles of their hands. This way of moving is known as **knuckle-walking**.

Walking upright

Chimps can also walk upright on their back legs for short distances. Chimps sometimes walk upright if they are carrying an object or when the ground is wet. They do not like putting their hands down on soggy ground.

Able to grasp

Chimpanzees have five fingers, including a thumb, on each hand and foot. Like all great apes, chimps have **prehensile** hands and feet. Prehensile hands and feet are able to grasp. Chimps hold on to branches, vines, and other objects with their fingers and thumbs.

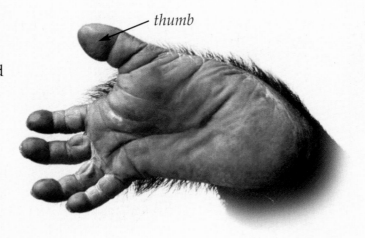

thumb

13

A chimpanzee's life cycle

Every animal goes through a set of changes as it grows. These changes are called a **life cycle**. A chimpanzee's life cycle begins when it is born. A mother chimp usually gives birth to one baby.

A newborn chimp is tiny. As it grows, the newborn becomes a **juvenile**. The juvenile continues to grow until it is **mature**, or an adult. An adult chimp is ready to mate and have babies.

Chimpanzees live for many years after they are mature. They can live for 40 to 50 years in the wild.

A newborn chimp weighs about two to four pounds (1-2 kg). It drinks milk from its mother's body.

Female chimpanzees are mature at thirteen to fourteen years of age. Males are mature between ten and thirteen years of age.

A chimp becomes a juvenile at about five years of age. It no longer nurses. A juvenile spends most of its time playing!

14

Always near

Young chimpanzees stay close to their mothers for the first five years of their lives. Mother chimps protect their babies. They carry their babies wherever they go. The babies hold onto their mothers.

Teaching the babies

Mother chimps teach their babies many skills, such as how to find food and how to build nests. If a mother chimp dies, another adult female chimp may care for her baby. This female then becomes the baby's mother.

Playful animals

These two chimps are grooming each other.

Chimps are social and playful animals, especially when they are young. They spend a lot of time **grooming**, or cleaning, one another. They groom one another by searching through each other's hair to pick out bugs and dirt. Grooming helps chimps feel comfortable with one another. It also helps them stay healthy.

Chimp sounds

Chimpanzees use different sounds to **communicate**, or send messages to one another. A hoot that starts softly and gets louder is one type of greeting. A long scream means "danger." When a chimp has found food, it lets out a loud, excited hoot. What message might this chimp be sending?

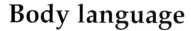

Body language

Chimpanzees also use their bodies to communicate. They shake hands, hug, tickle, and kiss one another. When chimps are angry, they sometimes throw things. They may shake sticks or other objects in an angry way. After a fight, chimpanzees sometimes hug to make up.

Finding a meal

Chimpanzees spend many hours each day eating. They are **omnivores**. Omnivores are animals that eat both plants and other animals. A chimp's **diet** is made up mainly of leaves, fruits, roots, and nuts. Chimps sometimes eat insects and small animals, as well.

Hunting in groups

Male chimpanzees hunt small animals such as monkeys, wild pigs, and small antelopes. The strongest males in a community usually catch the most animals. Chimps sometimes hunt alone, but they usually hunt in groups. A hunting group often splits into two smaller groups to catch an animal. One group chases the animal toward the other group. The other group then catches it.

Using tools

Chimpanzees are able to use tools to get food. A chimp "fishes" for termites or ants by dipping a stick into a termite nest or an anthill. When the chimp pulls out the stick, it is covered with insects, and the chimp licks them up!

These young chimps have found insects inside a mound of dirt. They will use a stick to gather the insects.

fishing for termites

Having five fingers helps a chimpanzee pick up and hold tools, such as the stick shown right.

Smaller habitats

One of the greatest threats to chimpanzees is the loss of their habitats. In Africa, the human **population** is growing faster than almost anywhere else in the world. To make room for farms, cities, and roads, people **clear** forests. To clear is to cut down all the trees. When people clear forests, they destroy chimpanzee habitats.

20

Nowhere to go!

People have built roads and cities in chimpanzee habitats. Roads and cities make it hard for female chimps to travel safely to other communities when they are ready to mate. Female chimps travel to other communities to find new males.

Many chimpanzees in a community are related. If female chimps mate with close relatives, their babies may not be healthy. The babies of closely related chimps may catch illnesses more easily than the babies of chimps that are not related.

Chimpanzees are hunted

Each year, many chimpanzees are killed by **poachers**. Poachers are people who hunt and kill animals **illegally**. Some of the chimps that poachers kill are eaten by **loggers**. Loggers are people who cut down trees for a living.

Money for meat

Other chimpanzees are killed so their meat can be sold to restaurant owners. Poachers kill many chimps because they can sell chimpanzee meat for a lot of money. There are laws against hunting endangered animals, but some people continue to break these laws.

Selling babies

Some poachers want to capture baby chimpanzees and sell them as pets, but mother chimps guard their babies well. To take the babies, poachers must kill the chimpanzee mothers, as well as any other chimps that try to protect the babies. For every baby taken, poachers may kill as many as ten adult chimps!

Not good pets

Baby chimpanzees are small and cute, but they are wild animals that should not be kept as pets. They need special care and become large, strong animals when they grow up.

Most people who buy chimps get rid of them when the chimps get older. The chimps often end up in small zoos. The workers at these zoos may not be able to care for the chimps properly.

23

Fewer chimpanzees

The chimpanzee population is very low, mainly because humans hunt chimps and destroy their habitats. Another reason there are so few chimps is that chimps do not have many babies. Female chimps do not begin having babies until they are over ten years old. The females then care for each baby for five or six years. During this time, they do not have other babies. Most female chimps have only three babies in their lifetimes.

Fewer babies

Some chimps are killed by poachers before they reach the age of ten. The chimp population cannot grow if chimps are killed before they can have babies.

Deadly diseases

Chimpanzee populations also cannot grow when illnesses spread quickly through chimp communities. In the 1990s, the **Ebola virus** killed many humans and chimps. In some chimpanzee communities, more than half of the chimps died from this virus.

When many chimps die at the same time from an illness, it takes a long time for the chimpanzee population to grow again.

Safe areas

People around the world are working to help chimpanzees. Some chimpanzee habitats have been turned into **preserves**. A preserve is patrolled by **rangers**. Rangers are people who protect the chimpanzees and the other animals that live on a preserve.

Rangers also help sick or injured animals and try to keep them safe from poachers. Some preserve rangers were once poachers themselves. These rangers know all the ways in which poachers may try to capture and harm chimps.

In a preserve, chimpanzees have the food they need to survive, and they are free to roam safely.

Chimps in zoos

Many chimps live in zoos all over the world. People who work in zoos know how to care for the chimps and keep them healthy. Zoos are safe places where chimps can raise their babies. Zoos also allow scientists to study chimps and learn more about them.

Visits from people

Some people visit chimps in their natural habitats rather than in zoos. They pay for guided tours through the areas where chimps live. The money visitors spend helps protect and care for the chimps. It also makes people who live nearby want to keep chimps alive!

People travel to African rain forests to see chimpanzees in their habitat. These young chimps are hiding among the tall grasses.

27

People helping chimpanzees

Scientists are working to protect chimpanzees. Some scientists are studying chimps in the wild. They are learning about how chimpanzees behave and what they need in order to survive. The scientists often ask local people to help them with their research. Scientists also teach local people why it is important to protect endangered animals and their habitats.

This scientist is studying chimpanzees that are living on a preserve. By studying these chimps, the scientist will learn how to help all chimps living in the wild.

A champion for chimps

Dr. Jane Goodall is one of the most famous chimpanzee researchers. She has spent more than 30 years studying chimps at her research center at Gombe, Tanzania, in Africa. Dr. Goodall was the first scientist to discover that chimpanzees eat meat and use tools to find food. Today, the Jane Goodall Institute continues her work at the Gombe Stream Research Center and at many other sites. Dr. Goodall now travels around the world to share her knowledge of chimpanzees.

Making faces

A fun way to teach others about chimpanzees is to communicate like a chimp yourself! You don't have to learn chimp calls, though. Chimps also communicate with their facial expressions.

Use the images below to create your own chimpanzee masks with paper and paint. Wear the masks for your family and friends and ask if they can guess what the chimps are communicating!

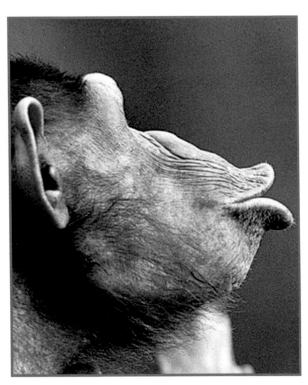

To greet one another, chimps make soft "hoo-hoo-hoo" sounds that build into loud "wha" sounds.

Are these chimps laughing, or have they found some food? Are the chimps making this face because they are scared? What do you think?

Knowledge on the Net

Can you help chimpanzees? The best way to help is to learn about chimps. You can then teach others what you have learned. You can learn about chimps from this book, other books, and on the Internet. Check out the fun chimp websites listed below.

www.panda.org—Click on "Species," then "Threatened species," "Great apes," and finally "Chimpanzees."

www.janegoodall.org—Learn about the Jane Goodall Institute.

www.nationalgeographic.com/kids—Click on "Creature Features" and then click on "Chimpanzees."

Glossary

Note: Boldfaced words that are defined in the text may not appear in the glossary.

clear To remove all the plants and trees from an area

diet The usual foods eaten by an animal

display The act of showing off by running around and making noise

dominant In control over others

Ebola virus A deadly disease that causes high fevers and bleeding

estimate To count approximately, not exactly

habitat The natural place where an animal lives

illegally Carried out against the law

mate To join together to make babies

population The total number of people or one type of animal living in a certain area

prehensile Able to grasp and hold things

preserve A natural area set aside by a country's government to protect the plants and animals living in that area

primates A group of mammals with large brains, including humans, chimpanzees, and monkeys

rain forest A thick forest in a hot region that receives at least 100 inches (2.5 meters) of rain per year

Index

1 2 3 4 5 6 7 8 9 0   Printed in the U.S.A.   4 3 2 1 0 9 8 7 6 5